The New York Colony

Bob Italia

ABDO Publishing Company

visit us at
www.abdopub.com

Published by ABDO Publishing Company, 4940 Viking Drive, Edina, Minnesota 55435.

Printed in the United States.

Cover Photo Credit: North Wind Picture Archives
Interior Photo Credits: North Wind Picture Archives (pages 7, 9, 11, 13, 15, 17, 19, 21, 23, 25, 27, 29)

Contributing Editors: Tamara L. Britton, Kate A. Furlong, and Christine Fournier
Book Design and Graphics: Neil Klinepier

Library of Congress Cataloging-in-Publication Data

Italia, Bob, 1955-
The New York colony / Bob Italia.
p. cm. -- (The colonies)
Includes index.
ISBN 1-57765-589-3
1. New York (State)--History--Colonial period, ca. 1600-1775--Juvenile literature. [1. New York (State)--History--Colonial period, ca. 1600-1775.] I. Title. II. Series.

F122. .I8 2001
974.7'02--dc21

2001022776

Contents

The New York Colony

Powerful Native American groups lived in the New York region before the Europeans arrived. The Dutch were the first Europeans to settle the land. But in 1664, the English took control.

The early New York colonists had to survive on their own. They made their own clothes and houses. And they grew their own food. Children helped their parents with chores on the farm.

At first, the colonists and the Native Americans got along well. But then they began fighting over land. Slowly, colonists forced the Native Americans from New York.

In the 1760s, the colonists grew angry with England. They disliked England's new laws and taxes. These disagreements led to the **American Revolution**. During the war, New York was the scene of many battles.

The colonists won the war. Then they formed the United States of America. New York became America's eleventh state in 1788.

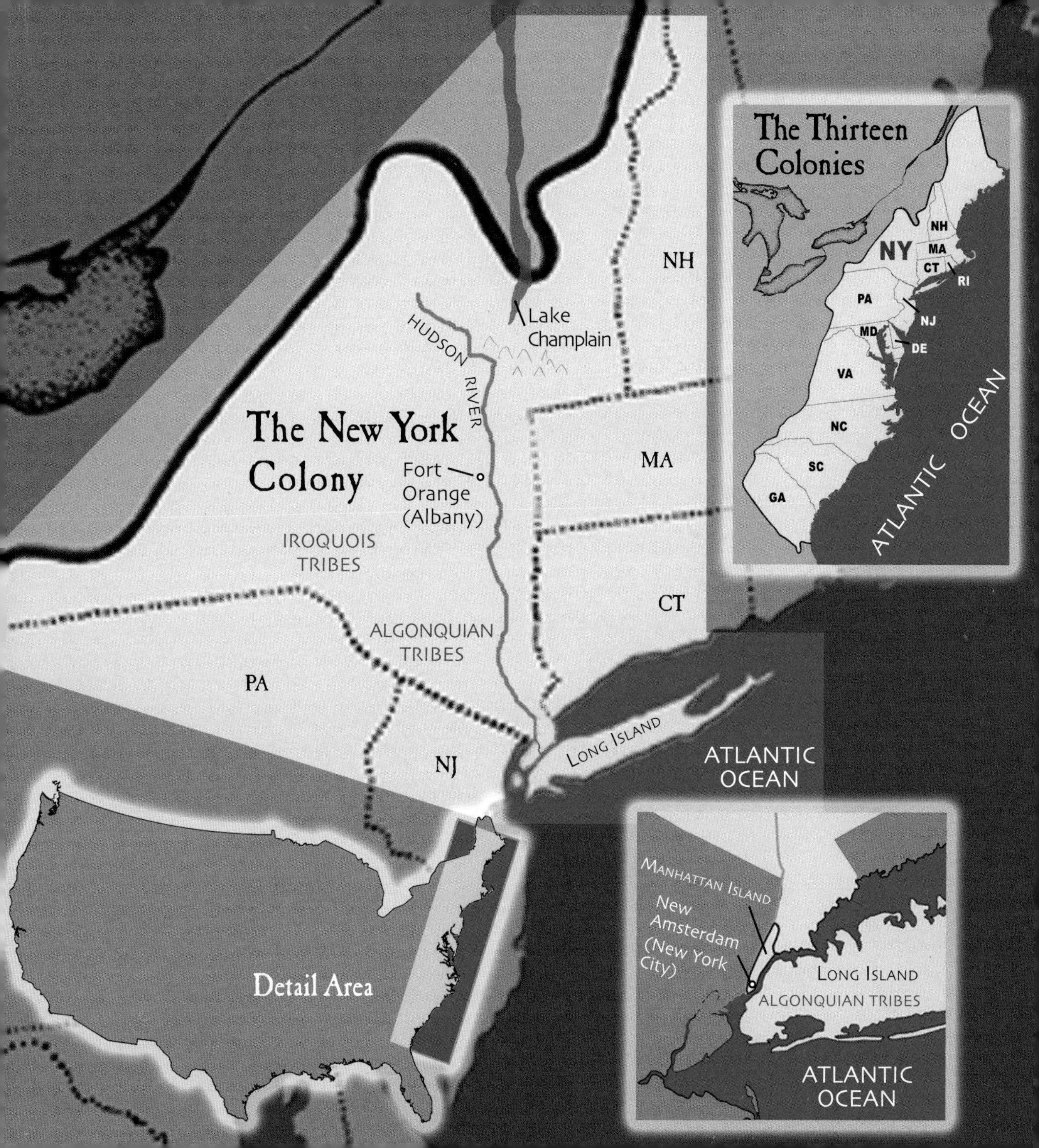
The New York Colony
Lake Champlain
HUDSON RIVER
Fort Orange (Albany)
IROQUOIS TRIBES
ALGONQUIAN TRIBES
NH
MA
CT
PA
NJ
LONG ISLAND
ATLANTIC OCEAN
The Thirteen Colonies
NY
NH
MA
CT
RI
PA
NJ
MD
DE
VA
NC
SC
GA
ATLANTIC OCEAN
Detail Area
MANHATTAN ISLAND
New Amsterdam (New York City)
LONG ISLAND
ALGONQUIAN TRIBES
ATLANTIC OCEAN

Early History

New York is located along the Atlantic Ocean. Its land has mountains, plains, and rolling hills. New York also has thousands of lakes and several important rivers.

Native Americans were New York's first settlers. Many powerful Native American groups lived in the area.

The Lenape, Mahican, Montauk, Munsee, and Wappinger all spoke **Algonquian** (al-GON-kwee-an). The Algonquian tribes settled in eastern New York. They lived in longhouses. They grew corn, beans, and squash. They also hunted and fished for food.

The Cayuga, Mohawk, Oneida, Onondaga, and Seneca were Iroquois (EAR-oh-kwoy). The Iroquois tribes lived in western and northern New York. They lived in bark cabins and longhouses. Their villages were often large and well protected.

A Native American village on Manhattan Island

The First Explorers

Italian explorer Giovanni da Verrazzano (gee-oh-VAH-nee dah ver-rah-ZAH-noh) sailed into New York Harbor in 1524. He was the first European to see the area. But then a storm came. Verrazzano had to leave without exploring the land.

In 1609, Frenchman Samuel de Champlain traveled into the New York area. He explored the land and discovered a large lake that was later named after him.

Englishman Henry Hudson also sailed into the New York area in 1609. He worked for the Dutch. They had hired him to find a shortcut to China. In search of this shortcut, he explored the large river that now bears his name.

Hudson never found the shortcut to China. But he did find a large, safe harbor and land with rich soil. When Hudson returned to Europe, he reported his findings to the Dutch. They quickly set up a fur-trading post there.

Henry Hudson's ship, the *Half Moon*, sails up the Hudson River.

New York's First Settlements

In 1621, a group of Dutch merchants formed the Dutch West India Company. It claimed the land in much of present-day New York, Delaware, Connecticut, and New Jersey. The company called its land New Netherland.

The Dutch West India Company sent its first colonists to New Netherland in 1624. About 30 families made the voyage. They were Dutch and **Walloon**.

Upon arriving, the colonists split up and started building settlements. One group founded Fort Orange along the Hudson River. It was the colony's first permanent settlement made by Europeans.

Another group founded a settlement on Manhattan Island. They called their settlement New Amsterdam. It had bark cabins, a fur-trading post, and a fort.

New Amsterdam quickly became the headquarters of New Netherland. The Dutch wanted to own the land. So in 1626, Governor Peter Minuet bought Manhattan Island from the Native Americans.

A group of Walloons lands at New Amsterdam.

Government

The Dutch West India Company operated the New Netherland Colony. The company appointed the colony's governor. In turn, the governor appointed a council. The council had the power to pass local laws and act as a court.

The Dutch governed New Netherland until 1664. That year, England's King Charles II sent soldiers to claim New Netherland. The colonists thought they had little chance of winning a battle against England. So they surrendered without a fight. New Netherland became an English colony.

King Charles II gave New Netherland to his brother James, Duke of York. The duke appointed Richard Nicholls as the colony's governor. A mayor, **alderman**, sheriff, and assembly helped Nicholls govern the colony.

The new government changed the name of the colony and its settlements. The New Netherland Colony was renamed New York in honor of the duke. The New Amsterdam settlement was renamed New York, too. And Fort Orange was renamed Albany.

Governor Peter Stuyvesant leads the Dutch troops out of New Amsterdam in 1664.

Life in the Colony

The first colonists had to survive on their own. Men built homes. They also cleared the land of trees and rocks so it could be farmed. Women prepared meals, tended their homes, and cared for their children.

Early on, the Dutch West India Company had a hard time finding colonists. The Netherlands was prospering. So few Dutch people wanted to leave their secure homes in exchange for a life in the rugged colony.

The company wanted the colony to expand. So it began accepting colonists of many different nationalities and religions. This made the colony the most **diverse** in America.

As the colony grew, social classes developed. The upper-class people were landowners, merchants, and government officials. Middle-class people worked as shopkeepers, craftsmen, and farmers. Lower-class people held jobs as laborers, soldiers, shop clerks, and servants.

A Dutch household in New Netherland

Making a Living

Early colonists traded with the Native Americans. They exchanged cloth, guns, and **trinkets** for furs. Furs quickly became valuable trade goods in the colony.

Colonists also worked on farms. They plowed the land and planted crops. Their crops included flax, rye, wheat, corn, vegetables, and tobacco. Farmers also raised livestock such as cows, sheep, goats, and pigs.

Not all colonists were farmers. Some worked in the shipping business along the waterfront. Others worked as printers, clockmakers, barbers, or tanners. A few women opened their own shops as **milliners**, dyers, or menders.

Some colonists used African slaves to help them in their businesses and on their farms. Slave trading became an important part of the colony's **economy**. Some colonists felt slavery was wrong, but it remained legal in New York until 1827.

Dutch fur traders on Manhattan Island

Food

Native Americans helped the early colonists. They taught them how to grow corn. Then they showed the colonists how to shell the corn, dry it, and pound it into meal.

Women prepared meals for their families. Colonists ate venison, goose, wild turkey, mutton, and raccoon. The colonists who lived close to the sea also ate fish and oysters.

Fruits were plentiful in the colony. In the summer, colonists ate melons. Women made jelly from wild grapes. They also picked peaches and apples, which could be eaten or made into cider.

Colonists eat dinner at a home in New Amsterdam.

Clothing

Rich colonists could buy their clothing from Europe. But most colonists did not have enough money to do this. So they had to make their clothes.

Women spun fibers from the flax plant into thread. They also spun wool shearings into thread. They wove the thread into cloth. Then the women cut the cloth and used it to make clothes. They sewed everything by hand.

Women wore dresses and aprons. Wealthy women could afford dresses made of silk, lace, and velvet. Common women wore dresses made of linen and wool.

Men wore kneesocks and short, leather pants called breeches. They wore linen shirts and fitted jackets called doublets. Some colonial men wore wigs, too.

In cold weather, men and women wore cloaks to keep them warm. Men also wore beaver caps, and women wore fur-lined hoods. Knitted mittens kept their hands warm.

These colonial women sew clothing for their families.

Homes

The early colonists made simple homes. They dug square pits into the side of a bank. Then they made a roof of sod and timber. They laid wooden planks on the floor. Inside, the houses were lined with bark to keep them warm.

Soon, colonists began to build small, one-story cabins. They made their cabins of logs or wooden planks. The cabins had fireplaces and thatched roofs.

After the colonists had become settled, they started to build larger, permanent houses. Many of these houses were made of brick. They often had two stories with steep **gables**.

When England controlled the colony, many of the houses were built in the English style. They were tall, square buildings. Many were two to three stories tall. They often had brick chimneys.

At first, many colonists made their own furniture. Homes had chairs, tables, and beds. Wooden boxes held linens and dresses. Meat safes stored salted meats. Later, colonists bought fine furniture for their homes.

A room inside a Dutch home in New York

Children

Religious groups founded most of the colony's schools. Classes were often held in a church. There, children learned spelling, writing, reading, arithmetic, and religion. Classroom rules were strict and punishment was harsh.

Wealthy parents sent their children to college in England or the other colonies. Then in 1754, New Yorkers started their own college. It was named King's College. Later, it was renamed Columbia University.

Though the colony had schools, few children could attend them. Children often had to stay home and help on their family farm. So their parents taught them to read and write at home.

Other children became **apprentices**. They could learn the skills they needed on the job. After working all day, some apprentices attended night school.

Children in the colony had time for fun, too. In the winter, children ice-skated on ponds and sledded down hills. In the summer, they swam or played games outside.

Colonial children play in their family's barn.

Native Americans

After taking control of the colony, England signed treaties of friendship with New York's Native Americans. But the colonists continued to take their land. And many Native Americans grew ill from diseases the colonists had brought over from Europe.

Beginning in 1689, New York suffered through four wars. During the wars, England and France fought for control of North America. **Algonquian** tribes aided the French troops. Iroquois tribes aided the English troops.

The last of these wars was called the French and Indian War. It began in 1754. New York was the scene of many battles. Many colonists and Native Americans died. England finally won the war in 1763.

Wars, colonial settlements, and disease hurt New York's Native Americans. Some tribes began to establish permanent villages outside their New York homelands. Others moved to **reservations** in New York and Canada.

Colonists sign a treaty with the Native Americans on Manhattan Island.

The Road to Statehood

After the French and Indian War, England sent many troops to protect the colonies. England's **Parliament** wanted the colonies to help pay for the troops. So it forced the colonists to pay high taxes on goods such as sugar, tea, and paper products.

Many colonists thought the taxes were unfair. They had no one to represent them in England's Parliament. So some colonists began to protest. This led England to attack the colonies in 1775. The attack started the **American Revolution**.

The New York Colony approved the **Declaration of Independence** in 1776. Then the colony formed a new government. In 1777, it approved New York's first state **constitution**.

During the war, colonists fought nearly 100 battles in New York. New York City fell to the English in 1776. But the next year, colonists won the Battles of Freeman's Farm. They were major victories for the colonies. They changed the course of the war in favor of the colonists.

The colonies officially won the war in 1783. Then they formed the United States of America. In 1788, New York approved the U.S. **Constitution**. This made New York the new nation's eleventh state.

Today, New York is an important state. It leads the nation in banking, communications, and finance.

New Yorkers protest England's high taxes.

TIMELINE

1524 - Giovanni da Verrazzano sails into New York Harbor

1609 - Samuel de Champlain explores the New York area; Henry Hudson explores the Hudson River

1621 - Dutch West India Company forms; claims New Netherland

1624 - First colonists arrive in New Netherland

1626 - Peter Minuet buys Manhattan Island from the Native Americans

1664 - England takes control of New Netherland; renames the colony New York

1754 - King's College founded; French and Indian War begins

1763 - French and Indian War ends

1775 - American Revolution begins

1776 - New York colonists approve the Declaration of Independence; English troops capture New York City

1777 - New York approves its first state constitution; colonists win Battles of Freeman's Farm

1783 - Colonists win American Revolution

1788 - New York becomes the eleventh state

Glossary

alderman - a member of a governing council.
Algonquian - a family of Native American languages spoken from Labrador, Canada, to the Carolinas, and westward into the Great Plains.
American Revolution - 1775-1783. A war for independence between England and its North American colonies. The colonists won and created the United States.
apprentice - a person who learns a trade from a skilled worker.
constitution - the laws that govern a state or country.
Declaration of Independence - an essay written at the Second Continental Congress in 1776, announcing the separation of the American colonies from England.
diverse - composed of several distinct groups of people.
economy - the way a colony uses its money, goods, and natural resources.
gable - the outside wall that is between the sides of a sloped roof. A gable is usually triangular in shape.
milliner - a person who designs, makes, sells, or trims women's hats.
Parliament - England's lawmaking group.
reservation - land set aside by the government for Native Americans to live on.
trinket - any small, fancy item such as jewelry or the like.
Walloons - French-speaking Protestants from Belgium and France. They left their homelands and moved to the Netherlands to escape religious persecution.

Web Sites

New York's Department of State Kids' Room
http://www.dos.state.ny.us/kidsroom/nysfacts/factmenu.html
This kid-friendly site is sponsored by New York's Department of State. It has a section on New York's history and fun facts. You can test your New York knowledge on the site's word search and crossword puzzle.

The New Netherland Museum
http://www.newnetherland.org/
Learn all about Henry Hudson's voyage on his ship the *Half Moon* at this site sponsored by the New Netherland Museum.

These sites are subject to change. Go to your favorite search engine and type in New York Colony for more sites.

Index